Aberdeenshire Library and Information Service
www.aberdeenshire.gov.uk/libraries
Renewals Hotline 01224 661511

KT-478-990

-7 JUN 2018

1 9 SEP 2023

1 4 OCT 2023

1 4 NOV 2023

1 9 DEC 2023

-9 MAR 2024

ABERDEENSHIRE
LIBRARIES
WITHDRAWN
FROM LIBRARY

ABERDEENSHIRE
LIBRARIES
WITHDRAWN
FROM LIBRARY

1 - DEC 2015

017

Ideri, Simona

ALIS

1898026

For Saul, SS
For Anne, SN

This edition published in 2003

Publisher: Anna McQuinn
Art Director: Tim Foster
Publishing Assistant: Vikram Parashar

First published in Great Britain in 2001 by Zero To Ten Limited
327 High Street, Slough, Berkshire, SL1 1TX

Copyright © 2001 Zero to Ten Limited
Text copyright © 2001 Simona Sideri
Illustrations copyright © 2001 Sheilagh Noble

All rights reserved.

No part of the publication may be reproduced or utilized in any form or by any means,
electronic or mechanical, including photocopying, recording or by any information retrieval
system, without the prior written permission of the Publishers.

A CIP catalogue record for this book is available from
the British Library.

ISBN 1-84089-274-9

Printed in Hong Kong

JP

Let's look at
FEET

Written by
Simona Sideri

Illustrated by
Sheilagh Noble

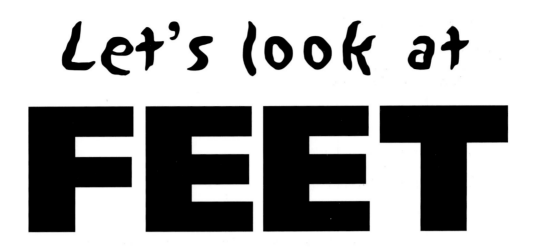

Look, feet are fantastic!

How many toes on each?

An elephant has five toes too.

But elephants' feet
are much bigger
than ours.

Horses have hard hooves.

Great for galloping!

Camels' feet are perfect for the desert.

They have
two toes
that spread
out flat,
so the camel
doesn't sink
in soft sand.

Birds' claws
are brilliant!

They curl round branches
and clutch tightly.

A duck-billed platypus
    has webbed feet
        to help it swim fast...

and dive deep.

Geckos
have sticky pads on their feet.

They can
cling on –
right side up
or upside down!

Feet are **fantastic!**

Some are fast and some are fancy...

but mine are best for me!

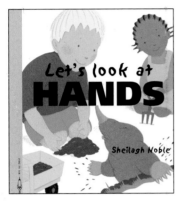

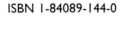
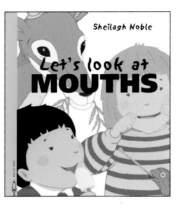

Hardback
ISBN 1-84089-145-9

Paperback
ISBN 1-84089-273-0

Hardback
ISBN 1-84089-144-0

Paperback
ISBN 1-84089-274-9

Hardback
ISBN 1-84089-147-5

Paperback
ISBN 1-84089-276-5

Hardback
ISBN 1-84089-146-7

Paperback
ISBN 1-84089-275-7

"SEARCH FOR THE ROCKET"

ZERO TO TEN publishes quality picture books for children aged between
zero and ten and we have lots more great books about animals!
Our books are available from all good bookstores.

If you have any problems obtaining any title, or would like to receive information about our books, please contact the publishers:
ZERO TO TEN 327 High Street, Slough, Berkshire SL1 1TX Tel: 01753 578 499 Fax: 01753 578 488

ABERDEENSHIRE
LIBRARY & INFO SERV

3026109

Bertrams	15/11/2010
JP	£5.99

Other Wibbly Pig books:
Wibbly Pig likes bananas
Wibbly Pig can dance
Wibbly Pig is happy
Wibbly Pig makes pictures
Wibbly Pig opens his presents
Wibbly Pig makes a tent
The Wibbly Pig Collection
Everyone Hide from Wibbly Pig
In Wibbly's Garden
Is it Bedtime Wibbly Pig?

First published in 2005
by Hodder Children's Books,

First published in paperback in 2006

Hodder Children's Books
338 Euston Road
London NW1 3BH

Hodder Children's Books Australia
Level 17/207 Kent Street
Sydney, NSW 2000

The right of Mick Inkpen to be identified as the author and
the illustrator of this Work has been asserted by him in accordance
with the Copyright, Designs and Patents Act 1988.

All rights reserved

A catalogue record of this book is available from the British Library.

ISBN: 978 0 340 89351 7
10 9 8 7 6 5 4

Printed in China

Hodder Children's Books is a division of Hachette Children's Books
An Hachette Livre UK Company.

Tickly Christmas, Wibbly Pig!

Mick Inkpen

Hodder
Children's
Books

A division of Hachette Children's Books

Wibbly Pig has a
Christmas scarf,
made last year,
especially for him,
by Big Aunt Larlie.
So it is very special.

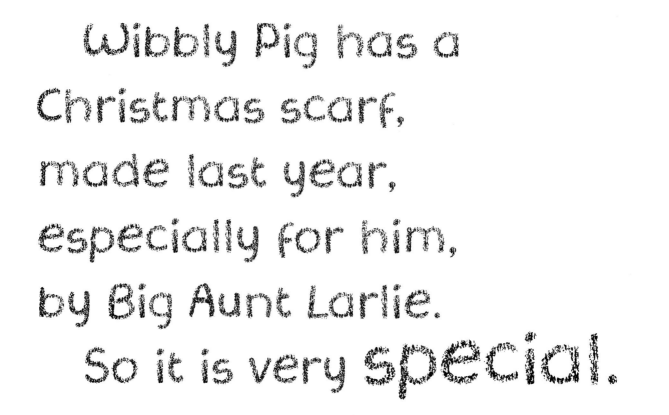

He doesn't like it
very much.

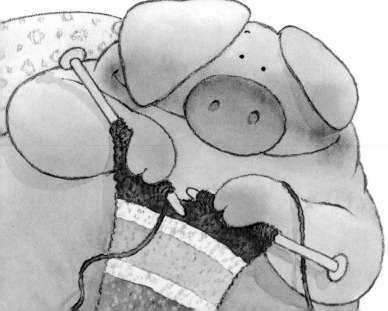

Wibbly has special gloves too. One of them arrived the Christmas before last.

And the other arrived the Christmas before that.
Can you guess who made them?

Big Aunt Larlie.

The Christmas before
all of these Christmases,
Wibbly Pig was just
a little, baby piglet.
And he looked
like this.

And Big Aunt Larlie
was to blame.

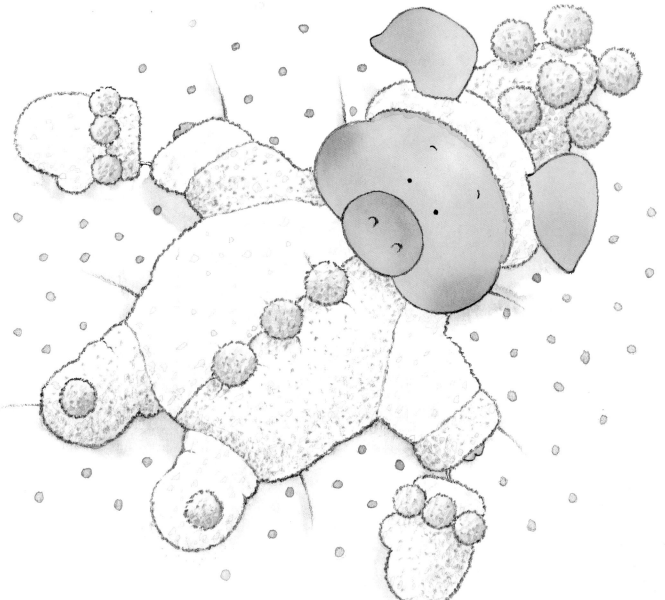

Wibbly's special scarf
and gloves are tickly.

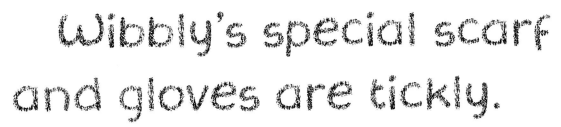

Itch!
Ooch!
Ouch!

But when it's cold outside,
and snow has fallen,
Wibbly Pig must wear his
special scarf, and his special
gloves. It's expected.

It is ten days before Christmas, and Wibbly Pig is helping to put up the Christmas decorations. This year, for the very first time, Big Aunt Larlie is coming to stay.

Big Aunt Larlie has bought herself some balls of wool – more balls of wool than usual.

Click! Clack! go her knitting needles.

Something very special is on the way.

Oh no.

Wibbly's friends do not have aunties like Big Aunt Larlie.

'I wonder what I will get this year,' says Wibbly Pig. 'I have tickly gloves. I have a tickly scarf.'

'I know!' says Spotty Pig. 'A tickly hat!'

It's Christmas Eve and
Wibbly Pig is investigating
Christmas parcels.
Itch! Ooch! Ouch!
The tree is tickly too!
Just like the hat he will
get from Big Aunt Larlie.

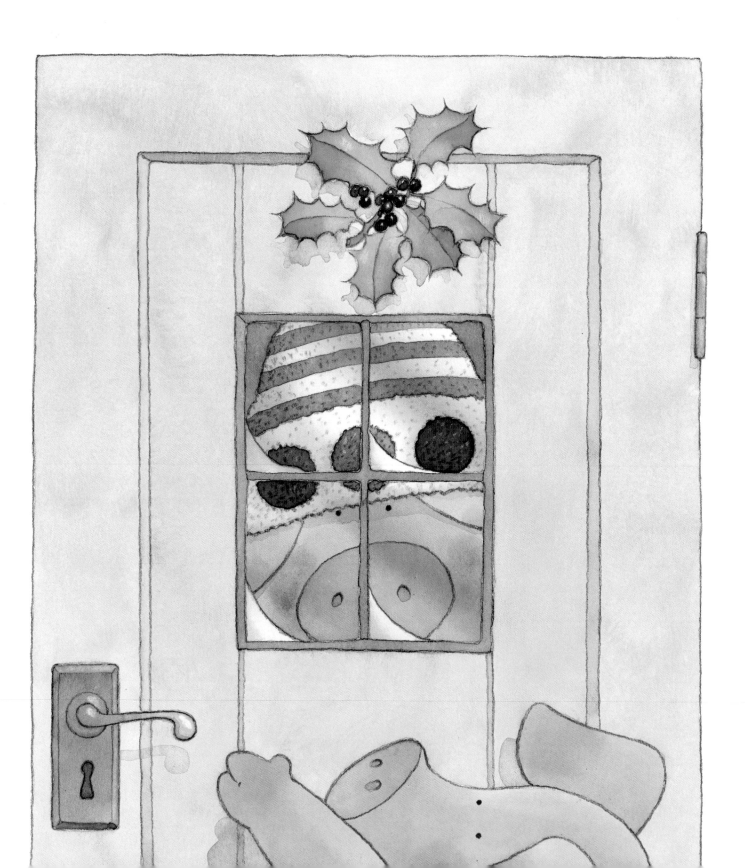

Ding! Dong! goes
the doorbell.
It's Big Aunt Larlie,
come to stay.

Wibbly Pig is
surprised.
'Aunt Larlie!' he says.
'You're wearing my
present!'

Big Aunt Larlie laughs.
'No I'm not, Wibbly
dear!' she says. 'This year
I've made a special
Christmas outfit for
myself!

This is YOUr present!'

There is no tickly
hat for Wibbly Pig!
Oh dear!
What a shame!

This year
Wibbly Pig
will have to
make do with...

...whooosh!

A toboggan!

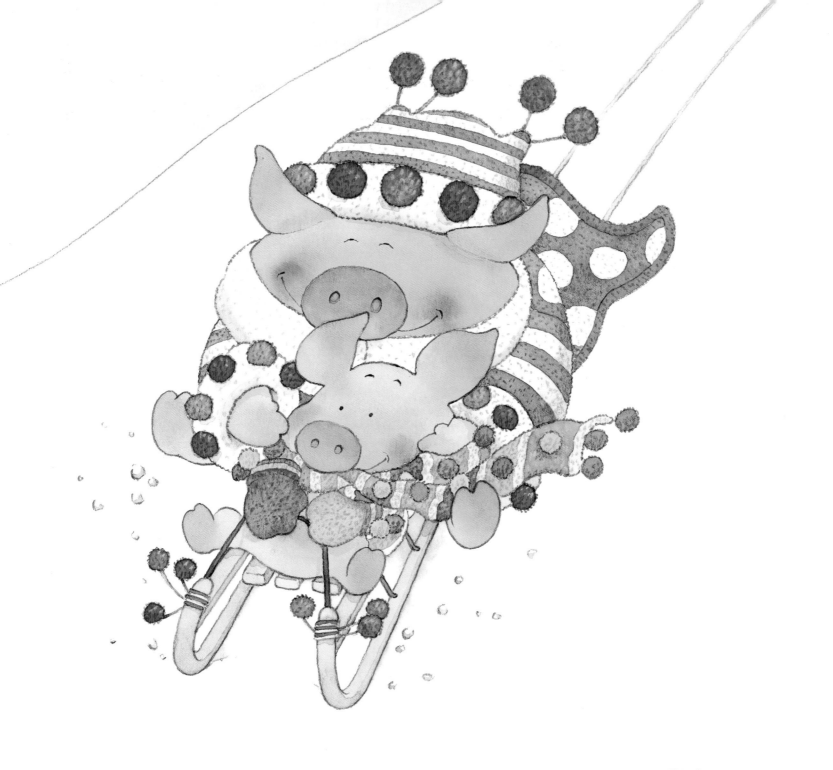

Happy Christmas, Wibbly Pig!